THINGS YOU SHOULD KNOW
(QUESTIONS AND ANSWERS)

By Rumi Michael Leigh

Introduction

I would like to thank and congratulate you for purchasing this book, *"Sociology, things you should know (questions and answers)"* series.

This book will give you a good knowledge about the human behaviour and how we react to what happens in our society.

Table of Contents

1) What is sociology?

2) What is socialisation?

3) What is a society?

4) What is the key to sociology research?

5) What is primary socialisation?

6) Name the agents of primary socialisation.

7) What is secondary socialisation?

8) Name an agent of secondary socialisation.

9) What is social representation?

10) Name two types of social representation.

1) Sociology is the scientific study of the human behaviour in relation to the society.
2) This is the process of the integration of an individual in a society.
3) A society is a group of people who live in a region and share the same culture.
4) Sociology searches the patterns, the recurring patterns between the human behaviour and the society.
5) This is the socialisation during childhood.
6) Family, school, etc.
7) This is the socialisation in which an individual is exposed to in all his/her adult life.
8) Professional socialisation.
9) This is an elaborated and shared social knowledge in the society.
10) Stereotypes and norms.

1) What is social location?
2) What are the main factors that determine an individual's social location?
3) Why is an individual's social location important?
4) Is sociology a science? If so, why?
5) What is history?
6) What is anthropology?
7) What is philosophy?
8) What is psychology?
9) What is social psychology?
10) What is paradigm?

1) This is the place where you fit in the society depending on several factors.

2) Race, religion, gender, sexual orientation, social class, etc.

3) It is important because it makes an individual know what he/she can do, his/her education, what he/she is allowed to do, his/her choices in life and limitations. And also, some factors beyond his/her control.

4) Yes. This is because it is also based on facts.

5) This is the research, knowledge of the past of humanity and human society.

6) This is the study of a human being in a holistic manner. It permits a person to know himself better.

7) It is the conception that consists of different principles of people and things.

8) This is a discipline that studies our mental activities and behaviour depending on the environmental conditions.

9) This is the interaction between the mental aspect of human and the social aspect.

10) It is a concept or pattern of how we analyse things, a situation, a topic, a subject.

1) What is critical sociology?

2) What is interpretative sociology?

3) Give an example of how interpretative sociology research is done.

4) What is a positive theory?

5) What is a normative theory?

6) What is subjectivity?

7) What is a quantitative research?

8) What is a descriptive data?

9) What is a qualitative data?

10) Name some ways of data collection.

1) This is a branch in sociology that studies the need and importance of change.
2) This is the branch of sociology that gives meaning to the human interaction with the society.
3) An interview.
4) This is a theory based on facts and it is a theory that is objective.
5) This is a theory that is not really based on facts and it is a subjective theory.
6) This is the meaning we attribute to things based on our way of thinking, our beliefs and experiences.
7) This is the research based on data.
8) This describes the data, evidence, facts, numbers, statistics, etc that are being researched.
9) This describes a data that normally cannot be quantified.
10) Experiments, observation, surveys and existing resources.

Leadership: Questions: Part 4

1) Who is a leader?
2) Name different types of leadership in a group.
3) What is transformational leadership?
4) What is charismatic leadership?
5) What is the main disadvantage of a charismatic leadership?
6) What is a transactional leadership?
7) What is a servant leadership?
8) What is an autocratic leadership?
9) What is a democratic leadership?
10) What is a bureaucratic leadership?

1) A leadership is the process a person directs/leads a group.
2) Transformational leadership, Democratic leadership, Charismatic leadership, Transactional leadership, Servant leadership, Autocratic leadership, Bureaucratic leadership, laissez-faire leadership, and Situational leadership.
3) A leadership that inspire, stimulates, builds confidence and use good communication skills.
4) A leadership that uses positive charms to stimulate and inspire the staff.
5) Since it is based on charm, the presence of the leader is often needed to stimulate the staff.
6) This is a kind of leadership that requires a sort of exchange. For example: there are rewards and punishments for tasks.
7) The leader shares his authority with the staff.
8) This is a sort of dictational leadership and only the opinion of the leader counts.

9) This is a sort of cooperation leadership; the leader is interested in the opinion of the staff before making a final decision.
10) This is a leadership based on hierarchy. The rules are highly regulated and must be strictly implemented.

1) What is laissez-faire leadership?
2) What could be the advantage of the laissez-faire leadership?
3) What could be the disadvantage of the laissez-faire leadership?
4) What is situational leadership?

1) This is when the leader leaves the staff with a high level of liberty.
2) It is good for creativity and already disciplined workers.
3) If the staff is not disciplined, it could cause disorganization, reduced productivity and even lack of respect between the staff.
4) This is when the style of leadership is adapted depending on the complexity of the situation.

Groups: Questions: Part 6

1) What are in-groups?

2) What are out-groups?

3) What is the main advantage of a small group?

4) What is the main disadvantage of a small group?

5) What is the main advantage of a large group?

6) What is the main disadvantage of a large group?

1) These are groups that we identify with.

2) These are groups that we don't identify with.

3) It has a solid bond.

4) It is less stable.

5) It is much more stable than a smaller group.

6) There is lesser bonding between the members of its group.

Social Economy: Questions: Part 7

1) What is capitalism?

2) What is socialism?

3) What is social stratification?

4) What is intragenerational mobility?

5) What is intergenerational mobility?

6) What is horizontal social mobility?

7) What is relative mobility?

8) Name the 3 main sectors of an economy.

9) What is the primary sector?

10) What is the secondary sector?

11) What is the tertiary sector?

1) This is a system that encourages making profit, competition and the resources in the economy are privately owned. This system is more about individual profit.

2) This is a system where the means of production are controlled by social ownership.

3) This is a way the society ranks people according to hierarchy.

4) This is the way an individual moves up and down the social ladder of the society during their generation.

5) This is the way an individual moves up and down the social ladder of the society from one generation to another.

6) This is when children work in a different occupation than their parents, but they still remain in the same or a similar social position.

7) This is the evolution in the social ladder compared to the rest of the society.

8) The primary, secondary and tertiary sector.

9) It is the sector that extracts raw materials from its natural environment.

10) It is the sector that converts raw materials into manufactured goods.

11) It is the sector that concerns making services of the primary and secondary sector.

General: Questions: Part 8

1) What is communication?
2) What are the common types of communication?
3) Name some channels of communication.
4) What are the factors that influence communication?
5) What is empathy?
6) Is giving advice, our own opinion part of empathy?
7) What are the imperatives of empathy?
8) What is sympathy?
9) What is compassion?

1) This is the transmission of message.
2) Verbal, non-verbal, written, digital information, etc.
3) Voice, gesture, light, facial expression, etc.
4) Hearing problems, age, level of education, language disorders, language barrier, social, and cultural origins.
5) This is the capacity to put oneself in another person's place, to understand what the person is going through by means of verbal or non-verbal communication.
6) No.
7) Active listening, accepting others without judgement, etc.
8) This is what one feels with others, one agrees with the persons feelings and participates in it.
9) This is a feeling of pity that makes us sensitive to the suffering of others.

1) What is a stereotype?

2) What are the functions of stereotypes?

3) Define prejudice.

4) What are the characteristics of prejudices?

5) What are the dimensions of prejudices?

6) Define discrimination.

7) Does prejudice always lead to discriminating acts?

8) What are some ways to fight against stereotypes, prejudice, and discrimination?

9) What are values?

10) What are norms?

1) This is a belief held by a person in relation to another person or group of people.
2) To explain reality, to give reality a sense, to rapidly treat information and Social justification.
3) This is a negative attitude often exaggerated towards a group or members of a group.
4) It brings a sense of affection (example: I don't like). It is generally associated with negative valences like sexism, racism, etc).
5) A motivational, an affective and a cognitive dimension.
6) This is a negative and unjustifiable behaviour against people that we have prejudice against.
7) No.
8) Finding a common goal. Learn to know oneself better and then learn about others. Experience the same situation.
9) Values are standards people use to choose what they perceive to be right or wrong or good or bad.
10) Norms are what we believe to be normal in a society.

1) What is marginalisation?

2) What is culture?

3) What is a symbol?

4) What are beliefs?

5) What are mores?

6) What is low culture?

7) What is high culture?

8) What is a counter-culture?

9) What is Ethnocentrism?

10) What is an aggregate?

1) This is when something is isolated and made to feel less important.

2) This is the way of life and the beliefs of a group of people.

3) A symbol is an object, shape, etc. that represents something, usually of value.

4) Beliefs are convictions.

5) These are norms, customs that are acceptable in a society.

6) This means the popular culture in a society. The culture observed by the majority of people in the society.

7) This is the non-popular culture in a society.

8) This is a culture that is opposed to the mainstream culture.

9) This is the judging of one culture by the standard of another culture.

10) These are individuals who are in a particular place at the same time.

Identity and Diversity: Questions: Part 11

1) What is a primary group?
2) Give examples of a primary group.
3) What are secondary groups?
4) What is deviance?
5) What is ideology?
6) What is stigmatisation?
7) What are the consequences of stigmatisation?
8) What is a correlation?
9) What is an empirical evidence?
10) Define status.

1) This is a small group that is very close. There could be emotional attachment and there is mutual support.

2) Family and friends.

3) They are large groups that have a common goal shared by every member in the group.

4) This is anything that deviates from what people consider as normal.

5) This is a system of ideas, beliefs, opinion of an individual or a group.

6) This is a process of discrediting an individual considered to be abnormal or deviant.

7) It makes the individual feel inferior/ the lack of self-esteem and it aims at giving another "image" to an individual.

8) This is when one event causes another event to follow.

9) This is a form of evidence where data is analysed by observation and/or by experiments.

10) This is the social position of an individual in the society.

1) What is patriarchy?

2) What is matriarchy?

3) What is gender stratification?

4) What are explicit biases?

5) What are implicit biases?

6) What is segregation?

1) This is a situation in a society where men dominate.
2) This is a situation in a society where women dominate.
3) This is the unequal distribution of resources across genders.
4) These are conscious beliefs or attitudes that we have about a group.
5) These are unconscious beliefs or attitudes that we have about a group.
6) This is a non-interaction of certain categories of people by physical and/or social separation.

1) What is social inequality?
2) Why do we use the word social in social inequality?
3) Who/what is the cause of social inequality?
4) Is it possible to fight against social inequality?
5) If the answer to question 4 is yes, then why?
6) What are the resources unequally distributed?
7) What is economy capital?
8) What is cultural capital?
9) What is social capital?
10) Define absolute poverty.

1) This is a situation where the resources of an economy are unequally distributed.
2) This is because the distribution of resources in an economy is a social phenomenon and not a natural phenomenon.
3) The social organisation of the society.
4) Yes.
5) This is because the organisation of distribution of the resources is done by people in the society.
6) Economic capital, cultural capital, and social capital.
7) This consists of all the economic resources of an individual which includes his salary and patrimony.
8) This consists of all the cultural resources of an individual which includes his level of education, skills, etc.
9) This consists of all the social resources of an individual which includes his social contacts and relationships.

10) This is the threshold of poverty. This includes the minimum necessary to survive.

1) What are the necessary needs for survival in the society?

2) What is the advantage of the definition of absolute poverty?

3) What is the disadvantage of the definition of absolute poverty?

4) What is relative poverty?

5) What is the advantage of the definition of relative poverty?

6) What is the disadvantage of the definition of relative poverty?

7) What is the principal vector of the reproduction of intergenerational social inequality?

8) What are some causes of social inequalities in the health system?

9) What are the consequences of constant social evaluations?

10) Name some health problems/dangers in relation to social inequality.

11) How can the social inequalities in health be improved?

1) Food, clothing, and shelter.

2) It shows the real measurement of poverty.

3) It does not allow international comparison.

4) This is a system of poverty that varies between one country to another.

5) It permits international comparison.

6) It depends heavily on the level of social inequality of a country.

7) Cultural inequalities, free tuition system and the school system.

8) The living conditions, somatic culture, the unequal health system, and the unequal social system.

9) Loss of confidence and an increase in anxiety.

10) Stress, obesity, drug consummation, violence, high prison incarceration and unwanted pregnancies.

11) Reinforce the health prevention campaigns and reduce the social inequalities.

1) What is health?

2) Is health the absence of illness?

3) What is public health?

4) What is a good health indicator?

5) Name the health indicators.

6) What is natality rate?

7) What is lethality rate?

8) What is an incidence?

9) What is a prevalence?

10) Define epidemiology.

1) This is a complete state of well-being, both physical and mental.
2) No.
3) This is a combination of technics and knowledge that help improve the health and quality of life in a population.
4) A good health indicator should be simple, easy to calculate, reproductible, valid and precise.
5) Life expectancy, Natality, Natality rate, Mortality, Mortality rate, Demography, Birth, Birth rate, Morbidity, Morbidity rate, Etc.
6) This is the total number of births (live births) in a population per thousand in a given year.
7) This is the number of people that contracted an illness and died of that illness per thousand in a given year.
8) This is the number of a new case in a population at a given period.
9) This is the total number of cases of an already existing illness at a given period.

10) This is the science that studies the frequency, the distribution and determinants of health and disease problems in a population.

1) What is prevention?
2) Give some measures of prevention.
3) What is primary prevention?
4) What is secondary prevention?
5) What is tertiary prevention?
6) What is health promotion?
7) What is screening?
8) What are the screening processes?
9) What are some important criteria of screening?
10) What is screening sensitivity?

1) Prevention helps to reduce illness impact or/ and stop its progression.
2) Improvement of the politics concerning health education. Environmental control. Medical intervention.
3) This is the prevention stage that aims at reducing the frequency of an illness.
4) This is the prevention stage that aims at detecting an illness at its early stages.
5) This is the prevention stage that aims at limiting the complications and progression of an illness.
6) This is a process that gives and encourages the population the means and control to improve on their health.
7) This is a clinical practice that helps to identify, test and treat illness in a population.
8) Determine the probability of illness in an individual. Give a diagnosis. Intervene if the diagnosis is positive.
9) The illness presents a major problem to the public health. The health benefits must be

superior to the physical risks. The screening process has to be acceptable by the population. The benefices of the screening must compensate or even better be superior to the economic cost to the screening. Etc.

10) This is the probability of having a positive result when the illness is present.

1) What is screening specificity?
2) What is the positive predictive value in screening?
3) What is the negative predictive value in screening?
4) Name some infectious illness that is checked with screening.
5) Name some cancerous illness that could also be checked with screening.
6) Name some other illnesses that could also be checked with screening.
7) What is systematic screening?
8) What is individual screening?

1) This is the probability to find a negative result when the illness is not present.

2) It is the probability that an illness is present when the test is positive.

3) It is the probability that an illness is not present when the test is negative.

4) HIV, Syphilis, Gonorrhoea, Hepatitis B and C, Tuberculosis (Pulmonary).

5) Breast cancer, Prostate cancer, Lung cancer, Skin cancer, Rectal cancer, Colon cancer.

6) Osteoporosis, Glaucoma, Cardiovascular diseases, Diabetes.

7) This is the screening intended for a defined population. A population in good health.

8) This is the screening intended in case of suspicion or signs of an illness.

Conclusion

Thank you once again for purchasing this book. I hope it has helped you gain more knowledge in sociology.

Please, if you enjoyed this book, I would like you to leave a review. It'd be appreciated.

Thank you.